DATE DUE

CONTEMPORARY AMERICAN SUCCESS STORIES

Famous People of Hispanic Heritage

Volume III

Barbara J. Marvis

A Mitchell Lane
Multicultural Biography Series
• Celebrating Diversity •

CONTEMPORARY AMERICAN SUCCESS STORIES
Famous People of Hispanic Heritage

VOLUME I
Geraldo Rivera
Melissa Gonzalez
Federico Peña
Ellen Ochoa

VOLUME II
Tommy Nuñez
Margarita Esquiroz
Cesar Chavez
Antonia Novello

VOLUME III
Giselle Fernandez
Jon Secada
Desi Arnaz
Joan Baez

VOLUME IV
Selena Quintanilla Pérez
Robert Rodriguez
Josefina López
Alfredo Estrada

VOLUME V
Gloria Estefan
Fernando Cuza
Rosie Perez
Cheech Marin

VOLUME VI
Pedro José Greer
Nancy Lopez
Rafael Palmeiro
Hilda Perera

VOLUME VII
Raul Julia
Mariah Carey
Andres Galarraga
Mary Joe Fernandez

VOLUME VIII
Cristina Saralegui
Trent Dimas
Nydia Velázquez
Jimmy Smits

VOLUME IX
Roy Benavidez
Isabel Allende
Oscar De La Hoya
Jackie Guerra

VOLUME X
Rebecca Lobo
Carlos Mencia
Linda Chavez Thompson
Bill Richardson

Publisher's Cataloging in Publication
Marvis, Barbara J.
 Famous people of Hispanic heritage. Vol. III / Barbara J. Marvis

 p. cm. —(Contemporary American success stories)—(A Mitchell Lane multicultural biography series)
 Includes index.
 LCCN: 95-75963
 ISBN: 1-883845-25-4 (hc)
 ISBN: 1-883845-24-6 (pbk)

 1. Hispanic Americans—Biography—Juvenile literature. I. Title. II. Series.

E184.S75M37 1996

920'.009268
QBI96-20404

Illustrated by Barbara Tidman
Project Editor: Susan R. Scarfe

Your Path To Quality Educational Material
P. O. Box 200
Childs, Maryland 21916-0200

TABLE OF CONTENTS

Acknowledgments

Every reasonable effort has been made to seek copyright permission where such permission has been deemed necessary. Any oversight brought to the publisher's attention will be corrected in future printings.

Most of the stories in this series were written through personal interviews and/or with the complete permission of the person, representative of, or family of the person being profiled, and are authorized biographies. Though we attempted to contact personally each and every person profiled within, for various reasons we were unable to authorize every story. All stories have been thoroughly researched and checked for accuracy, and to the best of our knowledge represent true stories.

We wish to acknowledge with gratitude the generous help of Elaine DagenBela of the Hispanic Heritage Awards for her recommendations of those we have profiled in this series. Our greatest appreciation also goes to Mari Vilar for her help in compiling our story of Jon Secada; Lucie Arnaz for her review of our story about and permission to reprint photographs of Desi Arnaz; and Giselle Fernandez (telephone interview May 17, 1995), Madeleine Teichmann (telephone interview May 23, 1995), and Evelyn Evans for their incredible patience, cooperation, and help in compiling our story of Giselle Fernandez.

Photograph Credits

The quality of the photographs in this book may vary; many of them are personal snapshots supplied to us courtesy of the person being profiled. Many are very old, one-of-a-kind photos. Most are not professional photographs, nor were they intended to be. The publisher felt that the personal nature of the stories in this book would only be enhanced by real-life, family-album-type photos, and chose to include many interesting snapshots, even if they were not quite the best quality. p.15, p.17, p.19 courtesy Giselle Fernandez; p.21 courtesy Madeleine Teichmann; p.29, p.31 courtesy NBC News; p.41 AP Photo/Guido Blandon; p.43 Bettmann; p.44 Globe Photos; p.45 courtesy Emilio Estefan Enterprises; p.49, p.50, p.52, p.54, p.60, p.62, p.64, p.65, p.66, p.67, p.68, p.69, p.70, p.71 courtesy Desi Arnaz personal archives; p.73 Globe Photos; p.82, p.84, p.86, p.87, p.90 UPI/Bettmann

INTRODUCTION

by Kathy Escamilla

One of the fastest growing ethno-linguistic groups in the United States is a group of people who are collectively called Hispanic. The term *Hispanic* is an umbrella term that encompasses people from many nationalities, from all races, and from many social and cultural groups. The label *Hispanic* sometimes obscures the diversity of people who come from different countries and speak different varieties of Spanish. Therefore, it is crucial to know that the term *Hispanic* encompasses persons whose origins are from Spanish-speaking countries, including Spain, Mexico, Central and South America, Cuba, Puerto Rico, the Dominican Republic, and the United States. It is important also to note that Spanish is the heritage language of most Hispanics. However, Hispanics living in the United States are also linguistically diverse. Some speak mostly Spanish and little English, others are bilingual, and some speak only English.

Hispanics are often also collectively called Latinos. In addition to calling themselves Hispanics or Latinos, many people in this group also identify themselves in more specific terms according to their country of origin or their ethnic group (e.g., Cuban-American, Chicano, Puerto Rican-American, etc.) The population of Hispanics in the United States is expected to triple in the next twenty-five years, making it imperative that students in schools understand and appreciate the enormous contributions that persons of Hispanic heritage have made in the Western Hemisphere in general and in the United States in particular.

There are many who believe that in order to be successful in the United States now and in the twenty-first century, all persons from diverse cultural backgrounds, such as Hispanics, should be assimilated. To be assimilated means losing one's distinct cultural and linguistic heritage and changing to or adopting the cultural attributes of the dominant culture.

Others disagree with the assimilationist viewpoint and believe that it is both possible and desirable for persons from diverse cultural backgrounds to maintain their cultural heritage and also to contribute positively and successfully to the dominant culture. This viewpoint is called cultural pluralism, and it is from the perspective of cultural pluralism that these biographies are written. They represent persons who identify strongly with their Hispanic heritage and at the same time who are proud of being citizens of the United States and successful contributors to U.S. society.

The biographies in these books represent the diversity of Hispanic heritage in the United States. Persons featured are contemporary figures whose national origins range from Argentina to Arizona and whose careers and contributions cover many aspects of contemporary life in the United States. These biographies include writers, musicians, actors, journalists, astronauts, businesspeople, judges, political activists, and politicians. Further, they include Hispanic women and men, and thus characterize the changing role of all women in the United States. Each person profiled in this book is a positive role model, not only for persons of Hispanic heritage, but for any person.

Collectively, these biographies demonstrate the value of cultural pluralism, and a view that the future strength of the United States lies in nurturing the diversity of its human potential, not in its uniformity.

Dr. Kathy Escamilla is currently Vice President of the National Association for Bilingual Education and an Associate Professor of Bilingual Education and Multicultural Education at the University of Colorado, Denver. She previously taught at the University of Arizona, and was the Director of Bilingual Education for the Tucson Unified School District in Tucson, Arizona. Dr. Escamilla earned a B.A. degree in Spanish and Literature from the University of Colorado in 1971. Her master's degree is in bilingual education from the University of Kansas, and she earned her doctorate in bilingual education from UCLA in 1987.

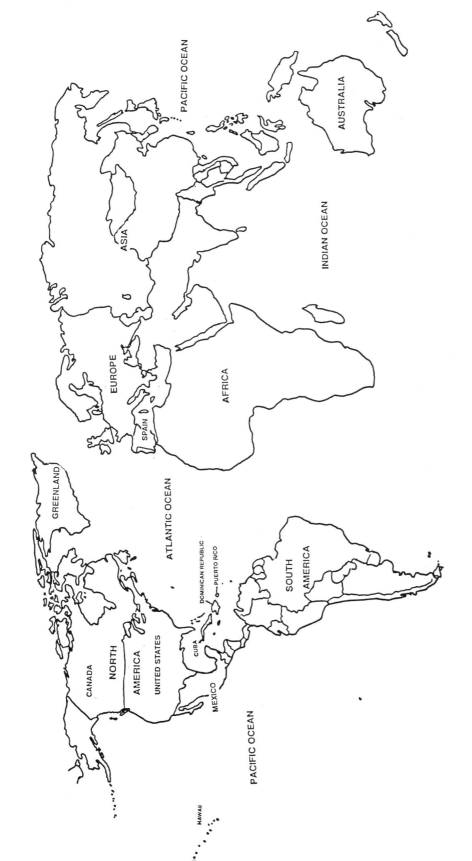

MAP OF THE WORLD

7

GISELLE FERNANDEZ

Reporter, Broadcast Journalist

1961-

"This business is about thinking clearly and writing. You don't have to be a genius to be a reporter, but you do have to have a natural curiosity and passion for life . . .**"**

Giselle Fernandez, as told to Barbara Marvis, May 1995

BIO HIGHLIGHTS

- Born May 15, 1961, Mexico City, Mexico; mother: Madeleine Eisner; father: José Fernandez; stepfather: Ron Teichmann
- Grew up around Los Angeles, California
- 1983, B.A. in Journalism from Sacramento State College, Sacramento, California
- Reporter and anchor for KRDO-TV, Colorado Springs, Colorado, 1983-1984
- Weekend anchor and reporter, KEYT-TV, Santa Barbara, California, 1984-1985
- Reporter and anchor, KTLA-TV, Los Angeles, California, 1985-1987
- Reporter and weekend anchor, WBBM-TV, Chicago, Illinois, 1987-1989
- Weeknight anchor and reporter, WCIX-TV, Miami, Florida, 1989-1991
- Correspondent and substitute anchor, CBS News, 1991-1995
- Currently: coanchor of NBC weekend editions of *Today* Show and anchor of the Sunday edition of *NBC Nightly News*. Living in New York.

"Good evening, everyone. I'm Giselle Fernandez reporting in New York. We have a breaking story to report for you."

GISELLE FERNANDEZ

She hangs up the phone and moves quickly to touch up her mascara. Comfortably seated in her chair on the studio set, she hears the familiar, "Okay, go!"

"Good evening, everyone. I'm Giselle Fernandez reporting in New York. We have a breaking story to report for you. Apparently there has been an explosion in Oklahoma City. Let's go live there now and talk with our reporter on the scene to find out the latest with what's happened. John, I understand there has been an explosion at the Federal Building. Can you give us an update of any information you have?"

Never at a loss for words, this bright, outgoing, people-oriented broadcast journalist is known professionally as Giselle Fernandez. An experienced reporter, correspondent, and moderator, she has learned to be ready at a moment's notice. She is always expecting the unexpected and is ready to cover or report any story the moment it breaks. Fresh out of college in the early 1980's, her rise through the local and network news ranks falls nothing short of phenomenal. In 1995 she became a coanchor of the NBC weekend editions of the *Today* Show and anchor of *NBC Nightly News*, Sunday edition.

Giselle Maria del Rocio Torres y Fernandez was born on May 15, 1961, in Mexico City. Known fondly by her family and friends as

GISELLE FERNANDEZ

"Gigi," Giselle was the second child born to Madeleine Eisner and José Fernandez. Her brother, José Antonio (Pepe), was born on February 17, 1960. She has a half sister, Antonia Fernandez, born in 1937 to her father and his first wife, Kathleen Burke. Her half brother, Joshua Teichmann, was born on April 9, 1975, to her mother and stepfather, Ron Teichmann.

Giselle's father, José, was born in 1900 in Irapuato, Mexico. His family was never wealthy. His father left when he was young, and his mother raised him by herself. He grew up with a great passion for the arts. He was married several times before he met and married Giselle's mother, Madeleine Eisner.

José had a long and illustrious career as a flamenco dancer, and he had made quite a name for himself in Hollywood during the 1930's. He worked for Paramount Studios during that time. A dynamic and energetic man, he was both a dancer and a choreographer. He danced at the Hollywood Bowl and was President of the Paramount Polo Club. As illustrious as his career might have been, however, he·was always a struggling artist. He used to dance at the Rainbow Room at Rockefeller Center in New York City, where Rockefeller loved to watch him. He often danced for royalty and the upper echelon of New York society. He got rave reviews, but

In 1995 she became coanchor of the NBC weekend editions of the *Today* Show and anchor of *NBC Nightly News*, Sunday edition.

From the time she was twelve until she was nineteen, Giselle's mother spent every summer in Mexico . . . She had immediately fallen in love with the small villages and towns . . .

GISELLE FERNANDEZ

he rarely had enough money in his pocket for bus fare home.

In 1931 he married Kathleen Burke, who had been a movie star. Kathleen and José had a daughter, Antonia, born in 1937. When Kathleen and José divorced, Kathleen took their daughter to live with her. José believed his daughter should be with him, so he took Antonia from her mother and crossed the border to Mexico, where he raised her with his next wife. Antonia never got a chance to see her mother until her later years. José married several more times before he met Madeleine in 1955.

Giselle's mother, Madeleine, was born on June 21, 1936, in New York City, to a comfortable middle-class family. Her family lived in various cities between New York and Texas while she was growing up. From the time she was twelve until she was nineteen, Madeleine spent every summer in Mexico. Never enamored with city life, Madeleine hated the oppressiveness of New York. She had immediately fallen in love with the small villages and towns she visited in Mexico. She loved their warmth, their music, their language, their art, and their culture.

Madeleine traveled to Mexico City for the first time when she was twelve. She took a tour with four other girls, chaperoned by a local woman, who organized the tour. Madeleine had a wonderful time during those two summer months. She nagged her mother to let her return the following summer. However, Madeleine's mother was not completely happy with the woman who had chaperoned the tour; so the following year Madeleine returned to Mexico with her mother's best friend, Norma, a teacher in New York. Norma had every summer free and she had no children of her own. Madeleine became her daughter for the summer, and Madeleine affectionately called her "Aunt Norma." For the first several summers, Aunt Norma and Madeleine lived in San Miguel de Allende, which was a small artist colony. Many people from the United States were attracted there, and the area grew. Aunt Norma met some friends who owned property about an hour and a half away in Tequisquiapan. They sold her some property there and she eventually built a house, where Madeleine then spent her remaining teenage summers.

After high school, Madeleine enrolled at Sarah Lawrence College in Bronxville, New York, and completed three years there. She also had been studying Spanish dancing at a school in New York during this time. One of the other students at the school was a wonderful dancer, but, the dancer confided to Madeleine, she had not learned to dance in New York. If Madeleine really wanted to be a good Spanish dancer, she

For the first several summers, Aunt Norma and Madeleine lived in San Miguel de Allende, which was a small artist colony.

In 1961, when her father was sixty-one years old, Giselle was born.

must go to Mexico and learn the art form there. So, much to her parent's chagrin, Madeleine dropped out of college in 1955 and moved to Mexico City to study Spanish dance.

In Mexico City Madeleine searched out the school that her friend from New York had recommended. The dance school was run by Carmen Burgunder, and Madeleine's teacher was José Fernandez. In love with the entire Latin culture, Madeleine was also attracted to this talented artist and craftsman. Though he was thirty-seven years older than she was (he was fifty-nine and she was twenty-two), the two were married in 1959. José's daughter, Antonia, was only one year younger than Madeleine. In fact, she and Madeleine became best friends over the years. But Madeleine's father never supported the marriage. (Her mother had died by this time.) Not only was he disappointed that she had married a man who was so much older than she was, but he also was upset that José had no means to support her.

In 1960 their oldest son, José, was born. The family called him Pepe. In 1961, when her father was sixty-one years old, Giselle was born. Giselle's mother recalls that they were not doing very well in Mexico City with José teaching flamenco dancing, and in 1962, when Giselle was just a year old, the family returned to Echo Park in Los Angeles, where José decided to try again to make a living in Hollywood.

Madeleine's father was thrilled to have her back in the United States, and, as incentive to get her to stay, he offered to help with finances if she would finish her college education. She finished her degree in Spanish and Mexican folklore at UCLA while she worked as a singing waitress to help pay the bills.

Giselle remembers those early years of her life. The family lived in a very small house where she and her brother had to share a bedroom. "We had no living room," Giselle recalls. "There was no couch. We had just a wooden floor with bars and mirrors and an old tape recording machine. My father's students would come to the house, and he would sit there in his black leotard teaching the people of California flamenco dancing. There were always dancers and other interesting people around, but my brother and I ran wild. My mother was out trying to earn a living because my father had too much of an artist mentality to do that. So my mother was singing Mexican folk songs in this restaurant where she worked as a waitress, and she was also working toward her Ph.D. at the same time. My mother used to go nuts when she'd come home

Dancing played a big part in Giselle's parents' lives.

▼▼▼▼▼

"My mother was really the pillar of the family; my father was just a lot of fun."

▲▲▲▲▲▲

at eleven o'clock at night and find we hadn't eaten. My dad didn't make us do any homework and there was no discipline. We ate beans every night. There was always a bottle of wine on the table and lots of animals in the house. We took in stray animals: we had dogs and maybe three cats . . .

"My mother was really the pillar of the family; my father was just a lot of fun." Giselle also remembers that, in addition to his talent as a dancer, her father was an artist who made castanets by hand. She still has a pair he made for her out of ebony.

Giselle attended the Rose Charlan Nursery School in Silver Lake. From her earliest days in school, Giselle had a talent for people. Her mother remembers that she always stood out. She was the little organizer – the little spark that ignited all the activities, even in nursery school.

Giselle entered Sherman Oaks Elementary School in Sherman Oaks, California, when she was five years old. Shortly after this, her mother and father's marriage fell apart; they were divorced in 1968. Madeleine took Pepe and Gigi to live with her and they visited their father on weekends. Giselle remembers that when her parents divorced, she blew up like a hippo. "My parents divorced and I got fat. I was a fat kid," she says. "The other kids would make fun of me, and I didn't have any cute clothes at the time. I was not the most popular kid in elementary school." All that changed, however, as Giselle grew older.

Her mother met a wonderful man, Ron Teichmann, at UCLA, where they were both getting degrees in Spanish. Ron spent a great deal of time with the family over the next several years. In 1971 Madeleine and Ron took Pepe and Giselle to visit a small village in southern Mexico called Tehuantepec. Before they left on their trip, Madeleine bought Giselle several long flowery skirts, which were in style at the time, from Bullock's, an expensive store in California. When they got to Tehuantepec, there were no rooms available. They finally found an old rooming house, but the rooms were so terrible, they all slept on the beach that night. In the morning, Madeleine and Ron went for a walk through the village. In the middle of the plaza, they saw Giselle dancing with some market children she had already made

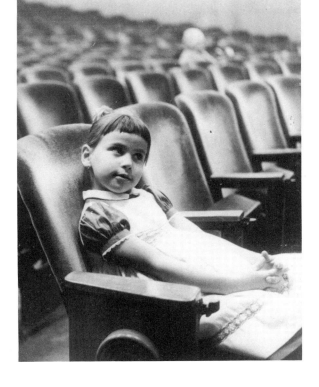

Giselle posed for this picture when she was about eight years old.

She wrote a wonderful composition about how she had made a large macramé bedspread for her four-poster bed, with a canopy to match.

friends with. "It looked like she was already best friends with these little girls," Giselle's mother recalls. "And Gigi went to the car, got out the brand-new skirts, and gave them to these children. The skirts that I had bought her looked just like their native clothing."

Giselle went to Patrick Henry Junior High School. She says she does not remember much of what happened before she got to high school, but her mother does. In 1973 Madeleine and Ron were married. Giselle's half brother, Joshua Teichmann, was born in 1975. Her mother remembers two incidents that took place when Giselle was in junior high that illustrate the type of "chutzpah" (guts) that Giselle has always displayed.

One day, Giselle's English teacher assigned the class to write about their greatest accomplishment in life. "Of course, they were only twelve years old," says Madeleine. "What did she think they had accomplished by this age?" Nevertheless, Giselle was never stumped by any assignment. She wrote a wonderful composition about how she had made a large macramé bedspread for her four-poster bed, with a canopy to match. Her teacher was very impressed by her accomplishment and asked Giselle to bring this bedspread to school to show to the class. Next thing her mother knew, there was an open house at school. All of the children's compositions were on display, and Giselle's teacher told Madeleine that she must be very proud of her daughter to have undertaken such a large project. "Well, this was news to me," says Madeleine. "I didn't know about any macramé bedspread, and I tried not to let the teacher know I was surprised by this revelation. But this was typical of Gigi. If her teacher wanted her to have a great accomplishment by the time she was twelve, she'd just make one up." The teacher continued to ask Giselle to bring in her bedspread, and Giselle eventually had to confess that she had made up the story.

Giselle and her brother, Pepe, posed for this picture, which was used on a book cover.

Another time while she was in junior high, the family was having dinner when Giselle announced that she had volunteered to play the piano for the chorus during their assembly in school that day. "That's very nice," said Madeleine to Giselle, "but you don't know how to play the piano. How did you do this?"

"Well," answered Giselle, "I've always wanted to play the piano, and since the chorus sings so loud, I just moved my hands all over to make it look like I was playing. No one even knew the difference because I was drowned out by all the singing!"

"I loved being president. I loved organizing things like the prom, fund-raisers, dances, and homecoming night."

GISELLE FERNANDEZ

In contrast to junior high, high school was great for Giselle. She attended Newberry Park High School in Newberry Park, California, which is north of Los Angeles and about sixty miles southeast of Santa Barbara. "This was a great phase of my life," remembers Giselle. "I was sophomore class president, junior class president, and then student body president in my senior year. I was the first [female] student body president in my high school. I was the loud-mouth clown and was not very good in school. By that I mean I got mostly B's instead of the A's my teachers said I should be getting if I applied myself. I got A's in English, C's in math, and B's in everything else. But I was a great organizer. I was totally involved. I loved being president. I loved organizing things like the prom, fund-raisers, dances, and homecoming night. I had a diversity of friends. I was never in one group. I was not with the jocks or the band or the cheerleaders, but I was included in all of them. I liked having access to all the people."

Giselle was involved in all the leadership events at school. She kept her hand in everything. And from these experiences, she decided she was interested in politics and wanted to make the world a better place. In 1979 she graduated from high school. Her graduating class voted her "best all around," and "most likely to succeed." They certainly were right.

When Giselle decided on a career in politics, she wanted to be close to the nation's capital, where she thought all the action was. She received a partial scholarship to Gaucher College in Baltimore, Maryland. In 1979 she enrolled there and chose a major in international relations. During this time, she was given a Lyndon B. Johnson scholarship internship with Barry Goldwater, Jr., who was her district representative in Washington, D.C. Giselle's experience was not a positive one. She says she was totally disillusioned by Washington life on "the hill." She met with considerable sexist remarks; she found there were more followers than leaders and very few visionaries. She decided that politics was not for her after all. Through her experience, however, she was introduced to the news media, and she was impressed by the reporters she saw. She thought she might like to become a reporter instead.

Giselle's family from top to bottom: Ron Teichmann, Madeleine Teichmann, Pepe, Giselle, and Joshua.

Giselle spent only one year at Gaucher College. "It was too expensive and I wasn't studying much," Giselle says. She transferred to Sacramento State in Sacramento, California, and enrolled her sophomore year as a journalism ma-

GISELLE FERNANDEZ

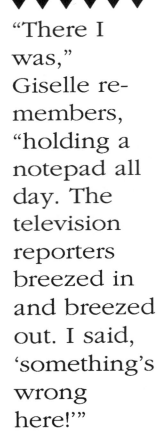

"There I was," Giselle remembers, "holding a notepad all day. The television reporters breezed in and breezed out. I said, 'something's wrong here!'"

jor. In 1983 Giselle was awarded a B.A. in Journalism with a minor in international relations.

During her three years at Sacramento State, Giselle worked as a reporter for the school newspaper, *The Sacramento Hornet*. She also worked for a brief time for a magazine called *Executive Place Magazine*. Since she was right at the California state capital in Sacramento, it was easy for her to cover news events there. When she would go to cover a story, she would see television reporters, who seemed to be having much more fun than she was. "There I was," Giselle remembers, "holding a notepad all day. The television reporters breezed in and breezed out. I said, 'something's wrong here!'" She decided that it would be much more fun to be in broadcast journalism. But most broadcast journalists have degrees in communications. She hadn't prepared for a career in front of a television camera, but now she wanted one. Never mind. She could fix that.

Giselle knew that she needed to make a videotape to send out to prospective employers if she were ever to break into television news reporting. She approached the communications department at her college and asked if they would help her make a tape. She wrote a story about merit raises for teachers to record on her video. Her biggest obstacle was what to wear.

Her family still did not have much money – they had two children in college – and Giselle wanted to be wearing a very expensive suit like all the other newscasters wore. She could not afford to buy one. Her mother remembers that this was no problem for Giselle, either. "She went to Robinson's, an exclusive local store, and picked out an outfit to wear," her mother tells us. "Then she went to the manager and convinced him to let her 'borrow' the outfit for just a few hours. Giselle told them she would not forget them when she became a successful journalist." The manager let her borrow the outfit!

Giselle sent out about one hundred tapes to stations all over the country. She got ninety-nine rejections. But there was one person in Pueblo, Colorado, who saw Giselle's tape and called her for an interview. Giselle says, "Keith Edwards called me and said: 'We'll fly you out here for the interview and pay for your plane fare if you take the job. If you don't take the job, you'll have to pay for half of your airfare.' He was looking for female Hispanic reporters and he really didn't care if I was any good or not. He just wanted a pretty face. I immediately said I'd take the job."

For Giselle's first job, she was hired as a reporter and photographer for the Pueblo bureau of the Colorado Springs station, KRDO-TV, an ABC affiliate. Pueblo, Colorado, is home to Colo-

Giselle sent out about one hundred tapes to stations all over the country. She got ninety-nine rejections.

"Some people say [that being Hispanic] is a point of discrimination," Giselle says. "But it is not. It got me in all the doors in this business."

rado Fuel and Iron (CF&I), which employed mostly Hispanic families. "Generations of families had worked in this steel mill," says Giselle, "which was the largest west of the Mississippi. They were closing parts of the mill daily and a lot of families were out of work. Main Street was starting to look like a ghost town, and a lot of my stories centered around CF&I." It was here that she saw her first drowning, saw her first dead body, and shot a camera for the first time.

Soon she was promoted to the KRDO headquarters in Colorado Springs. After about a year, Giselle missed home and she wanted to find a job back in California. She took a job at KEYT-TV in Santa Barbara, another ABC affiliate, as a weekend anchor and reporter. She did a lot of stories about immigration, health, and AIDS. Her first AIDS coverage was a profile about Ernie, who was dying from AIDS. It was very sad when she had to cover his funeral.

Since the immigrant population is so big in this area, Giselle found that being Hispanic was an asset. "Some people say it is a point of discrimination," Giselle says. "But it is not. It got me in all the doors in this business. It helped me get my jobs. It always put me ahead of the pack. Of course, after that, I had to prove I was competent in order to keep my job."

A story that Giselle covered in Santa Barbara turned out to be a critical point in her career. Her acquaintance with Fess Parker, who had portrayed Daniel Boone, later proved fortuitous in her climb to a major city reporter. Fess Parker lived in Santa Barbara and owned a ranch there. He was trying to convert the last piece of public land from parkland into commercial property along the beachfront. Giselle covered the story each day. There was a large immigrant population nearby who were poor and needed a public place to enjoy Santa Barbara. "It [Santa Barbara] was getting increasingly exclusionary and more expensive," says Giselle. Mr. Parker held a public referendum, which he won. He built the Red Lion/Fess Parker Resort and Convention Center, and left a small portion of the land as public park.

One day Giselle got a phone call from Hal Fishman, a famous anchorman. He said, "A friend of mine told me about you. He said you were quite good. We're looking for a Latina reporter. You should send me a tape."

Giselle asked, "Who's your friend?"

"Fess Parker is my best friend," answered Hal Fishman. So Giselle sent a tape and was hired as a weekend reporter for the independent station KTLA-TV in Los Angeles, her first major market. KTLA is the number-one independent sta-

GISELLE FERNANDEZ

"The bottom line is that I was always battling the fact that I was being hired because I was pretty and Hispanic."

tion in the country and is very well respected for its news coverage. From 1985 until 1987, Giselle worked in Los Angeles, where she got increasing recognition. She learned a lot, too. "People started to notice me," says Giselle. "Hispanic talent was very much in demand and I started getting job offers from all over. I had offers to go to New York, to Miami, and to stay in L.A." There was one offer Giselle liked a lot, however.

In 1987 Giselle went to Chicago to interview with Ron Kershaw, the news director at WBBM-TV. This was a very exciting time for her. She loved Chicago and was in awe of this talented news director. "The bottom line," Giselle says, "is that I was always battling the fact that I was being hired because I was pretty and Hispanic. When you're young and still learning your craft, you have to work three times as hard to prove yourself, not only to others, but also to yourself. You're always scrambling. Then as you keep gaining levels of competency, the old stereotypes stick. It's hard to contend with the insulting comments that you're hired only because you're pretty and Hispanic, especially once you've proven yourself."

Giselle worked very hard at her job in Chicago. She found she was trying to please her news director at every turn. "I was young and impressionable," she says, "and he spent a lot of time with me." In fact, Giselle said this might have been love at first sight. She had called her best friend in Phoenix shortly after she took the job and told her she had met the man she was going to marry! Giselle admits it is difficult to find someone compatible outside the business who wouldn't be completely taken with the glamour of TV. "People would always say, 'Oh, it's your news director.' But we worked together constantly. Because we're in the same business, we understand the [daily] pressures. You spend sixteen hours [together] in this place." And Ron and Giselle found they indeed had a lot in common; soon they were engaged to be married.

It was never to be. The year 1989 was a difficult one for Giselle. In July, Ron Kershaw died of pancreatic and liver cancer. He was only forty-three. One month later, in August, her father died from Alzheimer's disease. Giselle was devastated. She felt she needed to leave Chicago so she could get on with her life. She took a job in Miami as a weeknight anchor and reporter for WCIX-TV.

At first, the television managers thought it would be difficult for Giselle to adjust in Miami because she was not Cuban. But there was no problem at all. She was accepted right away. She anchored the 6:00 P.M. and the 11:00 P.M. news.

Two years later, Giselle landed her first network position: she was hired by CBS News in October 1991 as a New York-based correspondent and substitute anchor.

GISELLE FERNANDEZ

She covered the Persian Gulf War, the unrest in Haiti, the crisis in Cuba, and the U.S. invasion of Panama. She tackled a number of social issues that were widely reported on at the time, including homelessness, gay discrimination, and mothers on the run with their children. She covered much of the ethnic tensions between African Americans, Anglos, and Hispanics in Miami.

Two years later, Giselle landed her first network position: she was hired by CBS News in October 1991 as a New York-based correspondent and substitute anchor. She served as a substitute anchor on *CBS This Morning* for Paula Zahn; she substituted for Dan Rather on the *CBS Evening News* and for Connie Chung on the *CBS Weekend News*. In February 1992 she became a regular contributor to the *Eye in America* series on the *CBS Evening News* and took assignments for *CBS Sunday Morning, Face the Nation,* and *48 Hours.* She covered everything from Hurricane Andrew to the World Trade Center bombing. "It was a wonderful time," says Giselle. "I covered the biggest domestic stories." She loved being in the middle of all the news. She even went to Cuba and interviewed President Fidel Castro in October 1994. She was the first reporter to interview him in English in two decades!

When Giselle's contract with CBS was up, she found she had a number of options. She had several job offers from all three of the major networks. The opportunity at NBC gave her a chance to keep her hand in reporting. In February 1995 Giselle began a new job with NBC. "I miss being a full-time correspondent," she says. "I'm just learning my hosting duties, which are new to me. I'm trying to find a balance that will allow me to combine both into one job. I'm looking for a perfect blend of reporting and hosting. I have a four-year contract with NBC, and who knows what'll happen in the next four years. My goal is to find the proper niche. I don't want to be just a host, or just a correspondent, or just an interviewer. I don't know if what I'm about is out there yet. I'd like to do a little bit of entertainment, some programming . . . I need to find a venue that has diversity, which I don't think exists in today's news and entertainment. I'd like to do something that's a cross between [Dave] Letterman and [Ted] Koppel. I don't want to leave the news, and I don't want to be entirely in entertainment."

Giselle at her desk for NBC News

NBC reports that Giselle is expected to host a daytime program five days a week, beginning in early 1996. The program is now in development and Giselle is working with NBC to find

Giselle loves her career because it gives her access to the most interesting and fascinating people of our time. "I have a front-row seat to current history," she says.

GISELLE FERNANDEZ

just the right type of program – for her and for the viewing public.

Giselle loves her career because it gives her access to the most interesting and fascinating people of our time. "I have a front-row seat to current history," she says. "[My career] is my pass to go backstage beyond the velvet rope. I get to go beyond the yellow crime scene line. I get to experience the most amazing moments that define our times. I have had the opportunity to sit down and talk with Luciano Pavarotti, who has the most phenomenal voice of any tenor in the twenty-first century. I have had a chance to talk with Vice President Al Gore about issues I feel are important. I get to talk to leading scientists . . . Who else gets this kind of opportunity? I feel I have a front-row seat, and, to me, there is nothing more exceptional . . . As a woman, I take great pride in being able to cover a story with some sensitivity and a sense of cultural perspective. I can bring it to the nation my way."

Giselle's current assignment with *Today* requires her to get up at 4:00 A.M. to do her show at 7:00 A.M. She is really not a morning person, but she is sure she will eventually get used to the hours. She has generally enjoyed every challenge she has undertaken in her career. She finds the news business to be too rigidly formatted, however, and wishes there could be more flexibility in the coverage and scope of reporting. "I'd like to see a format that is more international in scope," says Giselle. "I wish it [to] be more diverse in terms of coverage of communities and cultures, the arts, and religious interests of our nations. I think we are much too limited in our perspective and approach. I think that international issues are news, not just when there is an explosion or high death toll. The world is much too small technologically these days to ignore trends and cultural diversity in other parts of the world; they should be a part of our domestic coverage, and I think someday they will be. We're just a little late in getting there. If I were to change anything [in this business], I guess it would be our very mid-America approach to the news. We are not a bland nation; we are not a narrow nation. Los Angeles, New York, and Washington are not the only corridors of news."

Still single, Giselle finds it difficult to establish a long-term relationship outside her business when her career keeps her traveling all over the world. With the changing shape of women's roles in the world, she is more than happy to wait for just the right person with which to share her life. She currently lives in New York. Like her father and her mother, Giselle loves to dance.

Giselle says that being pretty and Hispanic helped her get in the door. After that, she had to prove herself.

GISELLE FERNANDEZ

She takes modern dance and jazz lessons in New York City. She also takes piano lessons every week, so she no longer has to have a chorus singing to drown out her playing. She practices at least three times a week and is determined to learn to play the score for *Madame Butterfly*. She is also an accomplished ice-skater, and she used to compete. Of course, having been overweight as a kid, she runs every day. She says she runs in Manhattan about five miles every other weekday and seven miles on weekends. She is also a big reader and has a passion for autobiographies and for literature about women's lives.

Giselle says her mother will always be her best friend. Madeleine Teichmann currently lives in Westlake Village, California, with her husband, Ron, and youngest son, Joshua. Both her mother and stepfather are teachers at California Lutheran University in Thousand Oaks, California. They both teach Spanish; she teaches part-time; he teaches full-time. They are involved with multicultural activities on campus. Joshua has just completed his second year at Moorpark Junior College in Moorpark, California. He will enter Cal Lutheran in the fall of 1995. Giselle's older brother, Pepe, is married and teaches school in Capitola, California. He is also a basketball coach and an aspiring screenwriter. Antonia Fernandez

Giselle says her mother will always be her best friend.

is a longtime dancer and currently uses her dancing skills for New Age therapy.

For those who wish to follow Giselle to a career as a news reporter, she has this advice: "Be prepared to read as much as possible. If you want to be a reporter, there is no greater preparation than just reading. . . This will give you a broad-based tap on what's happening. . . If you read, you will become a wonderful writer. If you think clearly as a result of your reading, you'll be an even better writer. This business is about thinking clearly and writing. You don't have to be a genius to be a reporter, but you have to have a natural curiosity and passion for life. That's the essence of what will make you a good reporter."

Giselle's greatest asset is really her people skills. Her mother says she was just born with a natural talent for people. She has always had the guts and the drive to succeed. "Even with all her success," says her mother, "Giselle has not changed her being. Fame has not destroyed her. She is still the most wonderful daughter a mother could hope for."

"Even with all her success," says her mother, "Giselle has not changed her being. Fame has not destroyed her. She is still the most wonderful daughter a mother could hope for."

JON SECADA

Bilingual Recording Artist
1963-

"I 'm Hispanic but I'm also African. My roots are just as African as any black person who was born here. I consider myself a big melting pot of different cultures, which I want to attest to in my music. **"**

Jon Secada, 1995

BIO HIGHLIGHTS

- Born October 4, 1963, as Juan Secada in Havana, Cuba; mother: Victoria Secada; father: José Secada.
- Family fled Castro's Cuba in 1971
- Grew up in Hialeah, Florida
- Discovered singing talent when he was in high school
- Studied African-American jazz at the University of Miami; received bachelor's and master's degrees in jazz vocal performance
- Taught voice for six years at Miami-Dade Community College
- Signed with Emilio Estefan Enterprises in mid-1980's
- Married in 1988 to Jo Pat Cafaro; divorced in 1993.
- 1991, signed record contract with SBK Records
- 1992, released debut album, *Jon Secada*
- 1994, released second album, *Heart, Soul, & a Voice*
- 1995, appeared in *Grease;* chosen as AT&T's True Spanish Voice

JON SECADA

On June 17, 1994, musical megastar Jon Secada was honored to be singing at Chicago's Soldier Field for the opening ceremonies of the World Cup soccer tournament. Often referred to as "Miami Spice," or "Miami Nice," this unpretentious performer was ready to sing his latest hit, *If You Go*. His band began to play. Jon ran out on stage – and fell into a hole right in the middle of the platform. With TV cameras directed at him, he crashed to the ground, five feet below him. He dislocated his right shoulder and only his head was visible above stage level. He was in a lot of pain. So, what did he do on national TV? He burst into song, of course! He says the only thing he could think of at the time was the millions of people watching the broadcast, and he didn't want to be embarrassed in front of the whole world. Security guards had to pull him out of the hole.

Jon Secada, who became an overnight sensation in 1992, was born Juan Secada in Havana, Cuba, on October 4, 1963. He is the only child of Victoria, who is Hispanic, and José Secada, who is African. His parents ran a cafeteria in Cuba. But, after Fidel Castro's revolution, Jon spent much of his early years watching his parents struggle to get out of Cuba.

"Castro is a devil in disguise," says Jon. "There is no liberty in Cuba, no human rights.

Jon spent much of his early years watching his parents struggle to get out of Cuba.

My parents didn't want to raise me under that kind of government."

In 1966, when Jon was only three, his father tried to move the family legally to the United States. Castro wouldn't allow this, so José tried to escape by boat. He hoped to settle in Miami and send for his family. "But he got caught and went to prison for three years," Jon recalls.

In 1969, José applied again to leave legally. Castro sent him to a work camp for one and a half years, which was the punishment for all those who tried to get out of the country. After the paperwork was processed, the Secadas were finally allowed to leave in 1971. Jon was only eight years old when he flew from Havana to Miami. They had to leave everything they owned in Cuba.

"I have almost no memories of Cuba," says Jon. "I think it may be a block. We had to leave almost everything behind."

The Secadas settled in the largely working-class Hispanic area of greater Miami, known as Hialeah. They started a coffee shop there. "I grew up making Cuban coffee," jokes Jon. When he came to the United States, Jon remembers he was astonished to see the supermarket shelves bulging with food.

Jon was determined to make America his home. He threw himself into his studies. He was

In 1966, when Jon was only three, his father tried to move the family legally to the United States.

JON SECADA

a very good student. Though he never abandoned his native Spanish, he learned English quickly, mostly from watching TV, he says. His parents never did learn to speak English, however.

When Jon was a kid, he didn't listen to Latin music. "Most Cuban kids listened to disco and salsa; my instincts were more pop," Jon says. Even his childhood friends were mostly Anglos, and his music tastes were more for Stevie Wonder, Elton John, and Earth, Wind, and Fire.

When Jon was in eleventh grade, he discovered he had a talent for music. Though singing talent runs in his family (his Aunt Moraima Secada is a famous bolero singer in Cuba), Jon never gave music much thought. Then he sang the part of young Scrooge in a musical version of *A Christmas Carol*. "It was the first time the whole class heard his voice," says longtime friend and cowriter Miguel Morejon, "and everyone just said, 'What?'" His friends and teachers thought he had a great voice.

His teachers then encouraged him to further his career in music. Jon enrolled at the University of Miami, majoring in African-American jazz. He also spent a great deal of time mastering his skill at songwriting. He eventually earned a master's degree in jazz vocal performance and

When Jon was a kid, he didn't listen to Latin music.

began singing with local Top 40 bands. He played a lot of bar mitzvahs.

After he finished college, he took a job teaching voice at Miami-Dade Community College. Between his teaching career and his local performances, he was very happy. He didn't feel that his ambitions would extend anywhere beyond this. "The horizon for me was to be a working musician, which I was," says Jon.

One of his students at the community college was Jo Pat Cafaro, who was a freelance makeup artist. The two fell in love. They were married in 1988. After five years, the marriage ended in divorce, primarily, Jon says, because he married outside his culture. The language was a big barrier. "I didn't realize until I was with her how much speaking Spanish is a part of me. She couldn't cross over to my world," Jon says. "I always found myself translating. It just didn't work out."

In the mid-1980's, Jon met Emilio Estefan, who would change the face of Jon's career. Emilio had once been a marketing executive for Bacardi Rum, but he had had a different dream. At the time, he was also a keyboard player for a band called the Miami Latin Boys. Emilio met his future wife, Gloria, in 1978, and convinced her to join his band as their lead singer. Soon they changed their name to the Miami Sound Ma-

He eventually earned a master's degree in jazz vocal performance and began singing with local Top 40 bands.

chine and became a big hit. Emilio took a suite of doctor's offices on Bird Road in southwest Miami and turned them into a gleaming music factory. Emilio set out to make his wife a star.

Emilio was recruiting musicians for the Miami Sound Machine when two of Jon's college friends, who were associated with the Miami Sound Machine, passed Emilio a demo tape of Jon. Emilio liked what he heard, and since he had been looking for other artists to manage besides his wife, he signed Jon as an artist. Initially, however, he kept Jon in production.

For the next five years, Jon felt as if he had gone back to school. Emilio taught Jon every aspect of the music business. He toured, cowrote songs, and learned production skills and industry protocol. He helped produce music for Don Johnson and Pia Zadora. Then Emilio thought Jon should work directly with Gloria, which he did for the next three years.

In March 1990 there was a terrible accident. The bus carrying the Miami Sound Machine, including Gloria, Emilio, and their son, was involved in an accident with a tractor trailer on a snowy road in Pennsylvania. Emilio received only minor injuries, but Gloria broke her back. She spent the next year in therapy, recovering, and was unable to perform. For a period of time, she could not move. Gloria asked Jon to help

Emilio taught Jon every aspect of the music business.

her write two songs that later became number-one hits for her: *Coming Out of the Dark* and *Can't Forget You.* In 1991, when Gloria was finally able to perform again, she began her *Into the Light* world tour. Jon went along as a back-up singer.

Gloria wanted to help Jon break out from under her and win some recognition on his own. So, half-way through her concert performance, she gave Jon time to perform a solo. Throughout the tour, Jon had the opportunity

Jon is often mobbed for autographs. Here he is mobbed by a crowd of Cuban refugees at the Empire Range Camp #2 in the Panama Canal Zone in March 1994.

to sing in front of five million people in five different countries. His solo performance on Gloria's world tour led to his first record contract with SBK Records in 1991.

Jon was signed as an Anglo artist, but Emilio encouraged Jon to strive for a bilingual career. Emilio asked the record company to let them try two songs in Spanish on Jon's first album, entitled *Jon Secada.* So Jon made *Just Another Day*

"My career in Spanish was really overnight superstardom in every sense of the word," says Jon.

JON SECADA

(Otro día más) and *Angel* in Spanish. *Just Another Day* became a big hit, in both English and Spanish. It was one of the biggest selling singles in 1992, and it spent eleven consecutive weeks in the top ten of Billboard's Pop Singles Chart. The song made Jon an overnight star. His first album sold over six million worldwide; two million of those were sold in the United States.

"My career in Spanish was really overnight superstardom in every sense of the word," says Jon. "I didn't know I would get that kind of response from the Latin market. I'm very happy I did the Spanish songs, because, from day one, we've had both markets." This was a great accomplishment because the Latin market is musically diverse. The Hispanics in Miami don't necessarily like the same music as the Hispanics in Texas. It is difficult to satisfy this broad market, especially with pop music.

The Latin versions even crossed over into the mainstream market, Jon tells us, and became hits among the non-Latino population. "To this day," Jon says, "Anglos tell me that they might not understand what I'm singing, but there's immediately more passion in the Spanish versions of the songs."

Even though *Just Another Day* became a big hit, there were those who criticized it as being "Latin Lite." Jon responds, "I've never really thought of my music as being Latin. I write pop music with a bit of funk, soul, and undertones of Latin percussion." He describes himself as a product of Miami's complexity of cultures.

"Growing up in Miami gave me the freedom to mix all kinds of music," he says. He uses his Latino and African-American heritage as a springboard for multicultural music, which is not really Latin at all.

Since he became a star, Jon says his life has changed dramatically. "I didn't know what to expect when I sold all those records. I thought, Man, I'm going to be rich. But the fame! You touch people's lives. I had no idea how much."

Jon was nominated for a second Grammy for 1994. He is at a news conference in January 1995 with other nominees for the 37th annual Grammy Awards.

Jon writes most of his songs himself, often cowriting with longtime friend, Miguel Morejon. Jon's music is based on his own experiences with relationships. "Falling in love is cool," says Jon; "those initial moments of pleasure that you get from being with that person. You want to see [that person] every single moment of the day, and

JON SECADA

you have that person always in your mind." His marriage and divorce inspired many of his songs.

After the success of his first album, which included a Grammy for the Spanish version, Jon decided to change the direction of his music. In his second album, *Heart, Soul, & a Voice*, Jon chose to explore his rhythm and blues roots and his Afro-Cuban heritage. In connection with his new album, Jon made videos and did a tour that started on October 6, 1994, in Mexico City. In 1995 he toured in forty-two cities in the U.S. and Canada.

Jon holds the Grammy he won for the best Latin Pop Album of 1992.

With all his popularity, Jon was very busy in 1995. He was chosen by AT&T as their long-distance "true voice" for the Spanish language version of their popular commercial, which is shown on Spanish language TV in the United States and Puerto Rico. AT&T also sponsored his last tour. In addition, he recorded his third album, a collection of Spanish ballads released in the fall of 1995. Jon has also wanted to consider acting possibilities and was waiting for the right opportunity. He was cast as Danny Zukko in the Broadway production of *Grease*. In mid-June 1995, he traveled to Honolulu with the cast of *Grease* to perform there. Then he went back to

New York, where the show would be performed through the end of 1995.

Though the United States has been his home for most of his life, Jon still dreams of returning to Cuba to perform. His songs are played on the radio there, but they are not available for purchase in the stores. He still has a lot of relatives in Cuba, and if the island were ever to become free, Jon would like to go back.

For now, Jon wants to remain single. He is proud of his success and he feels obligated to serve as a role model for blacks and Latinos. "I want to be a good example, especially for young people," he says. What seemed like instant stardom to some was really the culmination of years of studying and hard work. Nevertheless, says Jon, "I'm living the American dream."

Jon is described by his friends as a nice guy.

DESI ARNAZ

Musician, Actor, Entrepreneur

1917-1986

❝I want to thank the United States of America and her people. I cannot think of another country in the world in which a young man of sixteen, broke and unable to speak the language, could have been given the chances to accomplish what I did, or the welcome, *cariño,* praise and honor which were given me. . . . **❞**

Desi Arnaz, *A Book* [William Morrow & Co., Inc., 1976]

BIO HIGHLIGHTS

- Born March 2, 1917, in Santiago, Cuba; mother: Dolores de Acha; father: Desiderio Arnaz II
- Family fled Cuba in 1934
- Desi finished high school in Miami at St. Patrick's High School
- First job with Siboney Septet as guitar player
- Xavier Cugat saw him perform and offered him a job with his orchestra
- 1937, Desi makes debut with band of his own; introduces La Conga
- 1939, starred in Broadway show *Too Many Girls*
- Met Lucille Ball while making the movie version of *Too Many Girls* in Hollywood
- Married Lucille Ball November 30, 1940; divorced 1960
- RCA Victor gave Desi his first recording contract for "Babalu"
- 1948, Lucy and Desi form Desilu Productions to coordinate all of their activities
- Lucie Desiree Arnaz born July 17, 1951
- First episode of *I Love Lucy* aired October 15, 1951
- January 19, 1953, Lucy gives birth to Desi Arnaz IV and "Little Ricky" on same night
- February 1953, *I Love Lucy* receives first Emmy
- 1957, Desilu purchases assets of RKO Studios, where Desi and Lucy had met
- 1962, Desi sells his shares of Desilu to Lucille Ball; Desi retires from public life
- Married Edith McSkiming, 1963
- July 1967, Desilu sold to Gulf & Western
- Died 1986

Desi, who grew up in Cuba, was the son of a wealthy landowning family.

DESI ARNAZ

I Love Lucy premiered on Monday, October 15, 1951, at 9:00 P.M. By the spring of 1952, *I Love Lucy* was the number-one show on the air. Lucille Ball and Desi Arnaz were suddenly the most famous couple in America. They made the cover of the May 26 issue of *Time*, and they were commonly called "Hollywood's Ideal Couple." By 1953, the couple had become so popular, they made the cover of *Life* one week and the cover of *Look* the next. In November they were invited to perform at the White House at the personal request of Ike and Mamie Eisenhower.

At first glance this might seem an unlikely outcome for a bongo-playing Cuban whose tongue could never get used to the English language. In fact, it was not. Desi, who grew up in Cuba, was the son of a wealthy landowning family. His father was mayor of Santiago, and little Desi enjoyed all the amenities in life. "The world was my oyster," Desi recalled. "What I wanted I only needed to ask for. Ambition, incentive, opportunity, self-reliance, appreciation of what I had meant little to me. I had a fast-swelling case of what in a language I couldn't speak at all then is called a fat head."

Desiderio Alberto Arnaz y de Acha III was born on March 2, 1917, in Santiago, Cuba. He was the only child of Dolores de Acha (known as Lolita) and Desiderio Arnaz II. His mother was a belle of high society, the daughter of one of the founders of the company that made Bacardi rum. His father was educated in the United States. He graduated from the Southern College of Pharmacy in Atlanta, Georgia, in 1913. He and Lolita were married in 1916.

In 1923, when Desi was just six years old, his father was elected the mayor of Santiago, Cuba's second most important city. His father was twenty-nine years old, the youngest mayor Cuba had ever had at the time. To Desi, his parents seemed like the king and queen – and he thought of himself as the crown prince. Desi grew up while Gerardo Machado y Morales was President of Cuba. Machado was backed by the American government, and, during his reign, Cuba became a favorable place for American investors.

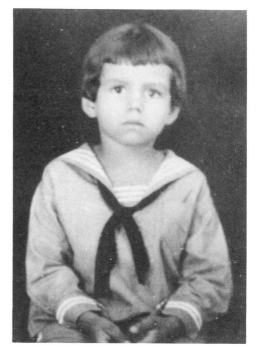

Desi when he was four or five years old

By his own admission, Desi had nearly everything he could want – except brothers and sisters. He was waited on by a staff of servants. He could go wherever he wanted in the mayor's mansion, as well as anywhere on the extensive

DESI ARNAZ

Arnaz property, which included a cattle ranch, two dairy farms, and a summer home on Cayo Smith, a little island in Santiago Bay. When he turned ten, his father and mother bought him a Tennessee walking horse. He owned a car and a speedboat long before he was legally old enough to drive them.

Desi when he graduated from grammar school

Desi was educated at strict Jesuit schools. He was expected to go to the United States for his college degree when he was old enough, just like his father before him. Desi says he would have rather been fishing or swimming. "All the high schools in Cuba are tough," recalled Desi. "Nevertheless, in my freshman and sophomore years I did have top grades — all A's, even in English, believe it or not. But in my junior year I was in real trouble with my studies . . ." That was the year Desi discovered girls.

In 1932 Desi's father decided to run for election to the House of Representatives from their province of Oriente. In June of that year, Santiago suffered a major earthquake. Desi and his mother were asleep at home, while

Desi's father was still at City Hall working on his congressional campaign. The rumbling woke Desi and he ran to his parents' room, where he found his mother praying. After the rumbling stopped, Desi returned to his room to get some clothes. He found that the wall behind his bed had collapsed and his bed was covered with bricks. He was lucky to be alive! Santiago suffered major damage during that earthquake, and about thirty people were killed.

His father was elected to Congress in November 1932, and in January 1933 he went to Havana to be sworn in. He had planned to move his family to Havana when he began his term, and a house was being built for them in El Vedado, an upscale suburb. One day Desi got an urgent call from his Uncle Eduardo telling him to get his mother and leave the house right away. "They're coming after you," he said. "Machado has fled the country and anyone who belonged to the Machado regime is in danger."

An economic crisis and public unrest led to the Cuban Revolution and the overthrow of Machado. Machado escaped to Miami, but he left the members of his government behind. They were all arrested and put into jail when Batista took over as the new President. Since Desi and his mother had received advanced warning from his uncle, they were able to go into hiding. But

Their house in Santiago was looted and all of their possessions were either stolen or burned.

their house in Santiago was looted and all of their possessions were either stolen or burned.

Their beach house and farms were also wrecked. Looters killed most of the animals and

Desi attended St. Patrick's High School in Miami. He is in the back row, far right.

left them to rot. Desi could not understand why any of this happened. His father had been a beloved mayor in his hometown. He asked his father, who was now in prison, how this could have happened. His father answered, "When so many people are hungry and don't have a decent place to live, medical care or good schools for their children, clean towns without flies and mosquitoes . . . they are apt to revolt."

Desiderio II remained in prison for six months. Since no charges were ever filed against him, he was let go. But he was advised to go to Florida until order could be restored in Cuba.

He borrowed five hundred dollars from relatives and went to the United States on a visitor's permit. It took three months for the family to be reunited. Desi came to the U.S. before his mother. When he stepped off the ferryboat in June 1934, he was seventeen years old. His father said, "*Bienvenido a Los Estados Unidos de Norte America*, and those will be the last Spanish words I will speak to you until you learn English." Desi tried to reply to his father in English, but, as he recalled, nothing too good came out. "Well, it will take a while for your ears to get used to it and for your tongue to handle it."

Desi later joked, "My ears eventually got used to it pretty well, but my tongue has been fighting a losing battle ever since."

Desiderio II started an import business with some other refugees. They had very little money of their own and they could not get credit. Desi and his father had to sleep in the warehouse, and after school Desi helped his father with the business. Desi also had to find many other paying jobs, such as cleaning birdcages, so he and his father could eat.

Desi attended St. Patrick's High School in Miami. He needed to take only one year of American History and English to graduate. He hung out with a group of rich kids. His best friend at that time was Al Capone, Jr., whose father was serving time at Alcatraz for tax evasion. The younger Capone and his mother lived in great luxury on an island off Miami Beach. Desi was often a guest.

Desi's first real job was with the Siboney Septet, a rumba band that played at the Roney Plaza. The band was looking for a guitar player, and, like most Cuban boys, Desi had been taught how to play the guitar. He auditioned for the band and was hired for thirty-nine dollars a week to play each night after school. Desi was happy to help his father out by making so much

The Siboney Septet had only six members, even with Desi.

money. But his father was not happy about this at all. He wanted Desi to go on to college and be a lawyer. "Oh no, my son is not going to be a . . . musician," said Desiderio II. Desi convinced his father it would help out with finances and it would be fun.

Desi ran into a worse problem than his father's disapproval, however. The immigration department found out that Desi was working almost as soon as he started. The immigration officer told Desiderio II that he and his son were not legal residents of the United States and therefore were not entitled to hold jobs. They had to apply to be permanent residents; that was the law. But the officer was a very understanding man. He told Desi's father that no one from the immigration department would show up at the Roney Plaza for three months. In that time, father and son were to get their papers in order to become legal residents.

Desi and his father could not apply to be permanent residents from within the United States. They had to go to an American consulate outside the United States to get their permanent residency papers. It was not safe for Desiderio II to return to Cuba, so he traveled to Puerto Rico. When he returned, Desi left for Havana to get his papers. Shortly after that, Desiderio II sent for his wife to come join them in the U.S.

Desi says he knew of no racial prejudice until he moved to Florida. The blacks in Cuba were his father's greatest supporters. "Our dances, for which we were as famous internationally as for our cigars, sugar, and Bacardi rum, were mostly African: the conga, rumba, and mambo," Desi said. "And our Cuban music, as Fernando Ortiz so lovingly put it, 'derived from a love affair of an African drum and a Spanish guitar.'" This was the music that Desi knew when he joined the Siboney Septet.

One day, shortly after Desi had returned to the United States from getting his residency pa-

Desi says he knew of no racial prejudice until he moved to Florida.

Desi
decided to
start his
own band
back in
Miami.

DESI ARNAZ

pers, Xavier Cugat, king of the rumba, saw Desi perform at the Roney Plaza. He told Desi he would like to give him a chance with his orchestra in New York and invited him to come audition. The next day Desi sang for Mr. Cugat, who offered him a job right away. But Desi said he could not come to New York until he graduated from high school. Desi had lost three years of school because of the Cuban Revolution. He had to earn his high school diploma before he would accept any job. Mr. Cugat told Desi to write to him when he graduated.

That June, Desi graduated from St. Patrick's High School. He was sure Xavier Cugat would have forgotten about him by then. He took a chance, however, and wrote to him. Cugat offered Desi one-way bus fare to New York to rehearse with the band and twenty-five dollars a week for a two-week trial period.

Desi's father was very much against the idea. His mother was on his side. "It's just like going to school, Dad," Desi tried to convince his father. "I don't know anything about the big-band business and I can learn a lot from Cugat. Besides, I've never been anyplace but Miami." His father finally gave in, and Desi was off for New York to meet Cugat at the famous Waldorf-Astoria Hotel. The orchestra was playing at the Starlight Roof. Desi rehearsed with the band and was offered a job starting at thirty dollars a week. Desi was absolutely thrilled to be associated with such a big-name band. He was going to open with the Cugat orchestra at Billy Rose's Aquacade in Cleveland, Ohio. Cugat taught Desi the importance of putting on a show rather than a performance. The Cugat orchestra was famous for its show, and Desi learned a lot.

After about six months, Desi decided to start his own band back in Miami. He felt he could not earn enough money with Cugat and he wanted to strike out on his own. Cugat told him, "You won't have a chance. There are not many people who know and like Latin music in this country yet." But Desi was determined to try. "Okay," Cugat eventually said, "I'll tell you what I'll do to get you started. You can bill yourself as Desi Arnaz and the Xavier Cugat Orchestra direct from the Waldorf-Astoria Hotel in New York City." Cugat offered to send Desi a band when he got some bookings.

On December 30, 1937, Desi's new band made its debut at a 250-seat club attached to the Park Central Restaurant in Miami Beach. The new place had no name. But Desi's band was so bad on opening night, no one was sure the place would ever need a name! Cugat had not sent Desi a coordinated group of musicians. Between them, they only knew two Latin songs. They

Desi
jumped up
onto the bar
and he did
a dance all
along the
top of it,
from one
end to the
other.

DESI ARNAZ

sounded terrible. The owner of the place, who had hired them for a six-week period, fired them after the very first night! Because they had a six-week contract, though, he agreed to keep the band on for the minimum two-week time, which was a union rule.

Desi realized he had to make a change quickly. The next night was New Year's Eve. Desi decided to try a conga, which was not well known in the United States at that time. But the beat was simple, and Desi spent all of the following day teaching it to his new band. That night, Louis Nicoletti (called Nick), who had left Cugat's orchestra in New York to manage Desi's new venture, went out on the dance floor and grabbed people to start a conga line. The people in the club had never heard of the conga before. They didn't know what was going on. But Desi played the drums and danced to the beat. Nick was on the dance floor hollering, "Folks, follow me." Desi was desperate. This had to work.

In a couple of minutes, people were on the floor following behind Nick. Then Desi jumped up onto the bar and he did a dance all along the top of it, from one end to the other. Then he jumped back onto the dance floor, and pretty soon he had the whole club doing a conga line. The people had so much fun that night, they told their friends about the new nightclub and the new dance. People came from all over. After about a week, the club was jammed every night. The owner was ecstatic and decided he wouldn't fire Desi after all. "Hey, Desi," he said, "how about calling the room Desi's Place?"

"No," replied Desi, "let's call it La Conga."

The sign went up the next day. According to Desi, that is how it all began. Desi and his band were hired for twelve weeks, the entire Florida tourist season. Between New York and Florida, Desi was able to keep his band working for the next several years.

In the summer of 1939, Richard Rodgers and Larry Hart, a musical-comedy writing team, saw Desi perform in New York. They offered Desi a part in their next Broadway show, called *Too Many Girls*. One of the characters in the show was a Latin boy about nineteen years old. The actor had to be able to sing and dance as well as act. Desi was hired to play Manuelito, one of four football players hired to protect a millionaire's daughter when she enrolls at college in New Mexico. At the time, there were not many Latin actors around. Even though Desi knew nothing about the theater, he decided to accept the job. The show debuted in New Haven, Connecticut, home of Yale University. At the end of the first act, Desi did a conga version of

The people had so much fun that night, they told their friends about the new nightclub and the new dance.

the pep rally song, and it became a showstopper. The show opened at the Imperial Theatre in New York City in October 1939. Desi also worked at the New York Conga during the show's run, and the club supplied him with a limousine to take him back and forth.

In late 1939 Desi demonstrated the conga on a variety-show broadcast for the National Broadcasting Company (NBC). He made a guest appearance on television, which was brand new at the time. No one thought television had a chance. At that time, there were only about 120 TV sets in use. They cost $660 a piece, about the price of a car. Desi thought it was some newfangled gizmo that would never catch on.

Desi starred with Lucille Ball in *Too Many Girls.* Desi is standing to the right of Lucy.

Too Many Girls ran for 294 performances. Then Desi accepted an offer from RKO Studios to go to Hollywood to make a movie version of the Broadway show. Lucille Ball was also hired for the movie, and the two began dating shortly after they met.

On November 30, 1940, Desi and Lucy eloped. They drove to Greenwich, Connecticut, in between his shows at the Roxy.

"Eloping with Desi was the most daring thing I ever did in my life," Lucy later recalled. "I never fell in love with anyone quite so fast. He was very handsome and romantic." There were bets all over the country that the marriage would never last – even two weeks.

In 1941 the war in Europe had been intensifying. It was a difficult time for a young couple to start a life together. Lucy and Desi bought a new home in the San Fernando Valley in California. They wanted to name their house. By combining their two names, they christened their house Desilu. Little did they know, they had named much more than a house; they had named a future empire.

RKO Studios thought that Lucy and Desi made a cute couple, and they considered teaming them in a movie. They started looking for costarring roles. But, Desi's Cuban accent was so heavy that his movie roles were limited. Lucy used to make fun of the way Desi talked all the time. She called him "Dizzy" and imitated the way "thing" sounded like "thin" when Desi said it. Back in Hollywood, Lucy was better known than Desi, having starred in movies for many years before *Too Many Girls*. Desi did not like being considered second banana to his wife, so he decided to go back to work with his band. The State Department asked him to join a del-

RKO Studios thought that Lucy and Desi made a cute couple, and they considered teaming them in a movie.

egation of movie stars and entertainers being sent to Mexico City to promote President Franklin D. Roosevelt's Good Neighbor Policy. This policy was to make sure that the Latin American countries would become U.S. allies in case the war escalated to involve the United States. It was also meant to increase trade for American companies, which had lost a lot of export dollars while Europe, Africa, and Asia were embroiled in war.

By the time the U.S. became involved in World War II, Desi had applied to become a United States citizen, but his papers had not yet come through. As a result, he could not enlist in the U.S. Navy or any branch of the armed services. He was eligible to be drafted, however. He received his draft notice in March 1943, but he injured his knee in basic training and was classified for limited service. He ended up entertaining the wounded at the nearby Birmingham Hospital.

World War II did not really change American show business. After the war, the U.S. Department of Justice ordered all the major movie com-

This picture of Desi and Lucy was taken shortly after they were married.

panies to dispose of their theater holdings. They said the major companies were creating a monopoly in the industry. When the wartime restriction against manufacturing television sets was lifted, TV entertainment made great advances.

RCA Victor gave Desi a recording contract, and he recorded "Babalu" and "Brazil." When his band got a job as the resident orchestra on Bob Hope's weekly radio program, the sales of his new records greatly increased. As a result, RCA released a collection of eight songs by Desi for his first album, called *Babalu*.

The television era really got its start about 1948, when an estimated 750,000 television receivers were sold. By the end of 1949, there were more than four million sets in use. There were many new stations, daytime as well as nighttime broadcasts, and the first major news and entertainment programs. People who did not own TV sets went to houses of neighbors who did. About this time, Lucy and Desi formed Desilu Productions to coordinate all of their activities, which now had expanded into radio, TV, personal appearances, and music recordings, in addition to movies and the theater.

Lucy and Desi had been looking for a way to work together for a long time. They had their own separate careers, and they were forced to be apart too much of the time. They put together

▼▼▼▼▼
RCA released a collection of eight songs by Desi for his first album, called *Babalu*.
▲▲▲▲▲▲

DESI ARNAZ

a vaudeville comedy act that they took on the road together. In the act, Lucy pretended to want a job with Desi's orchestra, but she didn't know the first thing about music. She got a lot of laughs by calling her husband "Dizzy Arnizy" and by making fun of his thick accent. Lucy had also been doing a radio show called *My Favorite Husband* on CBS for years. In early 1950, CBS began to talk to Lucy about transferring the half-hour situation comedy to television. Lucy said she'd do it, but only if Desi could play her husband. Her husband on the radio show had been a typical American guy, tall and blond. Desi would never fit the part, so they decided to change the husband to fit Desi. By that time, both Lucy and Desi had established careers and each was making a lot of money. They had to give all of that up to risk a television show, when no one really knew whether the show would make it or not.

Lucy and Desi found William Frawley to play Fred Mertz and Vivian Vance to play Ethel Mertz.

The pilot for the new show was filmed before a live audience at CBS Studios in Hollywood on March 2, 1951. It was billed as *The Lucille Ball – Desi Arnaz Show*. Desi played a struggling go-getter named Larry Lopez, whose all-American wife, Lucy Lopez, dreamed of being in show business but really didn't have any talent. The concept for the show remained similar, but the names were changed to Lucy and Ricky Ricardo before the first episode aired in October 1951.

When Lucy and Desi made the pilot for their new show, Lucy was pregnant with their daughter, Lucie Desiree Arnaz, who was born on July 17, 1951, in Los Angeles. *(I Love Lucy* was due to begin production in September.) Lucy and Desi had been married ten years by the time Lucie was born. They never thought they would be blessed with the baby they had hoped for. Desi

Lucy and Desi with their neighbor, Bill Henry of the *Los Angeles Times*, and Little Lucie and Little Desi

wrote a song in honor of their new arrival called, "There's a Brand New Baby at Our House," which he wrote with composer-friend Eddie Maxwell. He performed the song for the first time on his CBS radio program called *Your Tropical Trip*.

"Little Lucie transformed our life," Lucy recalled years later. "To have a baby at the age of forty and after ten years of marriage seemed almost like a miracle. I believe that whatever success Desi and I had after that we owed to Lucie. She was our lucky charm."

Lucy and Desi found William Frawley to play Fred Mertz and Vivian Vance (Jones) to play Ethel Mertz. Lucy and Desi became Lucy and Ricky Ricardo. Desilu produced all the *I Love Lucy* shows, which continued to be filmed before a live audience, because Lucy was much better in front of an audience where she could instantly see their reaction and play it for all it was worth. Lucy and Desi were considered masters of the double-take and of timing.

Lucie's first birthday

By the end of November 1951, *I Love Lucy* was the sixteenth most popular television show in the nation. By January 1952 it had jumped to number five. By the spring of 1952, the show had become number one on the air. Lucy and Desi were suddenly the most famous couple in America.

I Love Lucy was based on exaggerated satire and slapstick. Lucy always had some harebrained scheme: she wanted to make Ricky show his undying love for her, she wanted to break into show business, she wanted to outdo one of her wealthier friends, or she wanted to squirm out of a predicament she had gotten herself into.

Lucy and Desi kept everyone in America laughing week after week.

By May 1952, Lucy was pregnant again. Desi convinced CBS to allow them to write Lucy's pregnancy into the show. The network did not like the idea and they did not want their viewing audience to see Lucy pregnant, but they gave in. CBS would not permit them to use the word *pregnant* on the show, so Lucy was "expecting." The script called for Lucy Ricardo to have a baby boy on January 19, 1953, on national television. The TV show had been taped several weeks in advance of the real event and was scheduled for broadcast on the closest Monday to Lucy's due date. On January 19, 1953, Lucille Ball gave birth to Desi Arnaz IV by cesarean section. The nation saw the birth of Little Ricky on the same night. Hundreds of thousands of women all over the country who were pregnant at the same time as Lucy wrote to her. After Desi IV was born, she received thirty thousand congratulatory telegrams and letters.

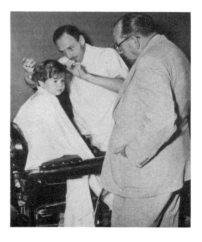

Grandpa Desiderio checks out Desi's first haircut.

In February 1953 *I Love Lucy* received its first Emmy from the Academy of Television Arts and Sciences. Desi not only acted in each episode of *I Love Lucy*, but he also supervised all the production details of the show and produced seven other Desilu series at the same time. In addition he dealt with other producers who used their Desilu studio.

At the beginning of each show, Desi would go on stage, in front of their live audience, dressed as Ricky Ricardo. He would then introduce Fred and Ethel Mertz, and then he'd say, "And here's my favorite wife, mother of my children, vice president of Desilu Productions, and the girl who plays Lucy – Lucille Ball!" *I Love Lucy* went on to win its second Emmy the next year, and 1954-55 was the third consecutive season that *I Love Lucy* was the most-watched show on television. In April 1955 the series was so popular, that CBS started doing reruns on Sunday nights, with new episodes airing every Monday evening. In October 1956 Lucy and Desi introduced Little Ricky on the show. What most people don't know was that little Ricky was not played by Desi Arnaz IV. He was not Desi and Lucy's real son. Instead, they hired Keith Thibodeaux, who adopted the stage name Richard Keith. He was a tiny drum player from Lafayette, Louisiana. Richard Keith came to live

Desi and Lucy with Tallulah Bankhead in a Lucy – Desi episode on the night they bought RKO Studios.

with the Arnazes while the show was in production.

The sixth season of *I Love Lucy* turned out to be its last. Early in the year, Desi had to be hospitalized when he tore some ligaments in his back while working on the set. The stress was also too much for Desi, and he decided that he should develop a show that Lucy could star in alone. Desi flew to New York to see William Paley, the chairman of the board of CBS. Paley agreed to a compromise that allowed Desilu Productions to do five hour-long specials called the *Lucy & Desi Comedy Hour*. It had special guest appearances by many Hollywood stars. One show aired each month beginning November 1957. They were to make a new weekly series for Lucy beginning with the 1958-59 season. On April 4, 1957, the Arnazes filmed the 179th and final episode of *I Love Lucy*. Their real children were on the show in bit parts.

In the fall of 1957, CBS gave the Monday night *I Love Lucy* time slot to another Desilu production, *The Danny Thomas Show*. (This show had previously been carried by ABC as *Make Room for Daddy*). About this time, Desilu Productions acquired the assets of RKO Studios, where Desi and Lucy had met, fallen in love, and worked in movies. Desilu now had thirty-five

Lucy finds uranium in one of the Lucy & Desi Comedy Hours with Fred MacMurray.

sound stages, plus an outdoor back lot of more than forty acres, making it the largest motion-picture and TV facility in the world at that time. In 1958, Desilu produced approximately 270 hours of filmed television entertainment – more than twice the footage of any movie studio. Desi Arnaz had become an entertainment tycoon.

Desilu Productions created *Desilu Playhouse*, and in the spring of 1959, it aired a two-part series called *The Untouchables*. The series was about Elliot Ness of the U.S. Treasury Department trying to wipe out mobsters Al Capone and Frank Nitti. CBS did not want the show, but ABC ordered twenty-six one-hour episodes for the 1959-60 season. It was later learned that the Cosa Nostra planned to assassinate Desi for producing *The Untouchables*. Desi was given a warning to cancel the show. He received a phone call from his old high school friend, Al Capone, Jr., who threatened to sue Desilu for $10 million for defaming the Capone family. The suit was later thrown out of court for lack of merit.

By 1959 the years of stress of running a large production company had put a terrible strain on Lucy and Desi's marriage. Desi wanted to sell the company and retire. Lucy wanted to continue working. The couple agreed it would be best if they divorced. Because they wanted to avoid

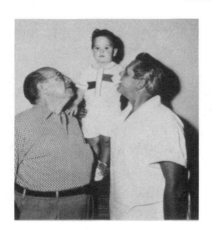

Three generations of the Arnaz family: Grandpa Desiderio with son Desi Arnaz and grandson Desi Arnaz IV

undue publicity, they agreed to a friendly separation. They even had the same attorney handle both their affairs. Lucy received custody of Lucie and Desi IV. All of Lucy and Desi's holdings were split down the middle. They had to divide their fifty-percent interest in Desilu, but they agreed that if one decided later to sell his or her remaining interest, the shares would be offered to the other one first. Even though they divorced, they were still tied to each other through their business and their children. They remained friends until Desi's death. They only appeared together in public however, at the annual company stockholders meetings.

The Arnaz family in the early 1950's

Desi said years later that as soon as *I Love Lucy* became a success, he wanted to quit the business. "Desilu had gotten to be a monster," he recalled. "In the beginning, it was fun. But when you're in charge of three studios with three

Desi said that *I Love Lucy* was much more than the name of a television show; it was his everlasting feelings for Lucille Ball.

thousand employees and thirty-five sound stages working all the time, the fun is long gone.

"The things that got me where I was I couldn't do anymore. I couldn't perform, I couldn't direct, I couldn't work with writers, I couldn't do anything but be a tycoon. I had bankers and stockholders breathing down my neck. I even had the FCC on my tail over *The Untouchables.* By that time, the show had gangsters of every ethnic group, including Chinese and Jews, so complaints were coming in from all over." And after more than a decade of being one of the most visible celebrities in America, Desi wanted to disappear from public view. He bought a forty-five-acre horse-breeding farm in Corona, California, and a vacation house in Baja, California. To keep Desilu in the family, Lucy exercised her right to purchase Desi's shares of stock. In November 1962 the board of directors voted to make Lucille Ball the new president of Desilu Productions.

In 1963 Desi married Edith McSkiming and disappeared from the celebrity limelight. Desi usually spent the weekends with his children. In 1966 Desi was sitting on the porch of his vacation house in Baja when the floor collapsed beneath him. He was flown to the Scripps Clinic in La Jolla, where an operation saved his life. But his health never returned to normal. He chose to live out the remainder of his life away from television and the media. Desi died in 1986.

In July 1967, Lucy sold Desilu to Gulf & Western, who packaged it together with Paramount Pictures. It then became Paramount Television. Lucy passed away in 1989, a few years after Desi.

Many of the shows that Desi produced in his lifetime are still in syndication and can be seen as reruns on various cable channels. Though the wonderful comedy team that started as a crazy redhead taking on a bongo-bashing Cuban is not alive any longer, it still lives on in the heart of Americans who are old enough to remember the enjoyment Desi and Lucy brought to every home each Monday night. Desi said that *I Love Lucy* was much more than the name of a television show; it was his everlasting feelings for Lucille Ball. Desi is certainly a shining example of the American dream come true.

Lucie and Desi, Jr., pose with their father in 1973 at La Costa Country Club in San Diego, California.

JOAN BAEZ

Singer, Songwriter, Social Activist

1941-

"Through all these changes my social and political views have remained astoundingly steadfast. I have been true to the principles of nonviolence, developing a stronger and stronger aversion to the ideologies of both the far right and the far left and a deeper sense of rage and sorrow over the suffering they continue to produce all over the world. **"**

Joan Baez, *And A Voice to Sing With* [Summit Books, 1987]

BIO HIGHLIGHTS

- Born January 9, 1941, Staten Island, New York; mother: Joan Bridge; father: Albert Baez
- Grew up mostly in California; lived for a year in Baghdad, Iraq, 1950-51
- 1959, debuts at Newport (Rhode Island) Folk Festival
- Recorded first album in 1960, Vanguard Records
- Met Bob Dylan in 1961
- 1964, toured with Bob Dylan; joined Martin Luther King's march from Selma, Alabama, to Montgomery
- Antiwar demonstrations, 1965 on
- Arrested for civil disobedience in 1967
- Married David Victor Harris, March 26, 1968; son Gabriel born December 2, 1969
- David Harris goes to prison for resisting the draft; Baez plays at Woodstock, 1969
- Joan and David divorce, 1973
- 1982, nuclear freeze demonstrations
- 1985, Live Aid concert
- Autobiography *And A Voice to Sing With* is published, 1987
- Currently: continues to perform live concerts; lives in Woodside, California

JOAN BAEZ

In 1964 the Vietnam War was escalating. Many Americans did not want the United States to be involved with the war. Some people protested loudly. Some refused to be drafted. There were antiwar rallies all over the country. Well-known folksinger Joan Baez decided to take a more radical stand. She learned that 60 percent of the national budget was being spent on the war. She declared that she would only pay 40 percent of her taxes. She wrote a letter to the IRS and sent the same letter to the news media. The letter was printed in newspapers all over the world.

One day an IRS agent showed up at Joan's house. He told her she was really being silly; why didn't she just pay up and avoid a lot of trouble? Joan invited him in for a cup of coffee. The agent refused and made her come to his office, where he continued to threaten her with jail if she did not pay the taxes she owed. Joan still refused. So the IRS put a lien on her house, her car, and her land. People from all over the country sent her checks, imagining that she needed the money to pay her taxes and that she was homeless. She continued to refuse to pay her taxes for ten years. Sometimes IRS agents would appear at her concerts and take cash from the registers. Eventually the government got all its money, plus the fines, but Joan insisted on

The IRS put a lien on her house, her car, and her land.

making it difficult and expensive for them to collect it from her. This was her nonviolent protest not only of the Vietnam War, but of all wars. Over the years, singer/songwriter Joan Baez has been as well known for her outspoken views and principles of nonviolence as for her music.

Joan Chandos Baez was born on January 9, 1941, in Staten Island, New York. She was the second of three daughters born to Joan Bridge Baez and Alberto Vinicio Baez. She has an older sister, Pauline, born in 1939, and a younger sister, Mimi, born in 1945.

Joan's mother, Joan Bridge, was born in Edinburgh, Scotland, and raised in the United States. Her mother died when Joan Bridge was only two. She and her older sister Pauline were raised by abusive stepmothers. Then her father became ill and died suddenly. Joan and Pauline Bridge were sent to separate foster homes.

Joan's father, Albert, came to the United States from Puebla, Mexico, when he was two years old. Albert's father was a Methodist minister who had been assigned to work with Brooklyn's Hispanic community. Albert had originally planned to become a minister like his father, but he later developed a passion for physics. He was working his way through Drew University in Madison, New Jersey, when he met and married Joan Bridge.

This was her nonviolent protest not only of the Vietnam War, but of all wars.

JOAN BAEZ

Albert Baez moved his family around the country and the world, though most of Joan's early years were spent in California. After he earned his degree at Drew, Albert moved the family to California. There he enrolled in a mathematics program at Stanford University and worked toward his master's and Ph.D.

While Albert was getting his Ph.D., the family owned a boarding house, where they rented out rooms to earn money. When Albert finished his degree, he took a job as a research physicist at Cornell University in Ithaca, New York, and moved the family back East, to a place about an hour from Buffalo.

Joan Baez remembers that music was always in their home. Her father would play Bach or Brahms or Beethoven. Joan took piano lessons and was always singing along with the songs on the kitchen radio. Her mother and father became Quakers early in their marriage. They raised their three children as Quakers, and the nonviolent religious beliefs have inspired Joan ever since.

At Cornell, Albert Baez became the head of Operations Research, which was involved in testing fighter jets. He could have stayed there and had a very profitable career. But, Joan tells us, her father was a pacifist, and rather than get rich doing defense work that he didn't believe in, he became a college professor. "We would never

Joan remembers that music was always in their home.

have all the fine and useless things little girls want when they are growing up," Joan recalled. "Instead, we would have a father with a clear conscience."

When Joan was in fifth grade, her family moved back to southern California, where Albert Baez took a job teaching at the University of Redlands. A year later, he took a job with UNESCO; he taught and he built a physics lab at the University of Baghdad. From 1950 to 1951, the Baez family lived in Iraq. Joan and her sisters were sick with infectious hepatitis most of the year they spent abroad. Joan saw animals being beaten to death, people searching for food in garbage pails, and legless children dragging themselves through the streets, begging for money. Her passion for social justice was born in this year in Baghdad.

At the end of 1951, the family returned to Redlands, California, where Joan entered junior high school. Joan recalls that she felt very isolated during these years. There was a large Mexican population where she went to school, but they were mainly immigrants and illegal aliens who came from Mexico to harvest crops. At school, they all gathered together and spoke Spanish. Joan spoke no Spanish, so she was left out of their groups. Because her name, skin, and

"We would never have all the fine and useless things little girls want when they are growing up," Joan recalled. "Instead, we would have a father with a clear conscience."

hair color were Hispanic, she was not accepted by the Anglos, either.

Her loneliness was an important factor in Joan's decision to become a singer. She thought she could be more popular if she sang, and she spent an entire summer developing her voice and learning to play the ukulele. She made her first stage appearance in a school talent show. She then taught herself to play the guitar by listening to famous singers such as Harry Belafonte. As her father accepted new teaching positions and Joan moved from school to school, she used her singing talent as a way to make new friends.

In 1958, after Joan turned seventeen and graduated from high school, the family moved again. This time they moved to a suburb of Boston – Albert Baez had taken a teaching job at the Massachusetts Institute of Technology. Joan agreed to attend the Boston University School of Drama, mostly to please her parents.

The family's new home was only a short distance from the Harvard Square area of Cambridge. Students from Brandeis and Harvard Universities would visit coffeehouses in Cambridge, where they would listen to folksingers, jazz musicians, and poets. A short while after they moved to Massachusetts, Albert Baez took his family to Tulla's Coffee Grinder, where folksing-

Her loneliness was an important factor in Joan's decision to become a singer.

ers often played. Joan loved the coffeehouse scene. She quickly lost interest in college and began spending most of her time in Harvard Square. She accepted an invitation to perform at Club Mt. Auburn 47, a jazz club there. People enjoyed her singing so much, she soon had offers to sing at other coffeehouses.

In 1959 Joan was popular enough to record her first album, *Folksingers 'Round Harvard Square*, which she recorded in a basement with two friends. She met popular folksinger Bob Gibson, who invited her to appear with him at the Newport (Rhode Island) Jazz Festival that August. Her performance at the festival was an overwhelming success; it launched her career.

In the summer of 1960, Joan recorded her first album with Vanguard, a small record company known mostly for its quality classical music. The solo album, entitled *Joan Baez,* was released around Christmas that year, and it soared to the number-three spot in the nation. About the time her record was released, Joan moved back to California. Her agent, Manny Greenhill, was not pleased about Joan's decision to return to California. Most of the concerts he was booking for her were in the East. In 1961 Joan traveled back East to give about twenty concerts. She was so popular that Coca-Cola offered her $50,000 to do an advertisement for them. She turned them

In the summer of 1960, Joan recorded her first album with Vanguard, a small record company known mostly for its quality classical music.

JOAN BAEZ

down flat: "I don't want to become a product," she said. But her phone was ringing day and night with offers for concerts and record albums.

Joan with Bob Dylan in London in 1965

Joan first saw folksinger Bob Dylan at Gerde's Folk City in Greenwich Village, New York, in 1961. She was not impressed. In May 1963 she went to hear him sing at the Monterey Folk Festival in California. After the performance, Joan and Bob became friends. They performed together at the Newport Folk Festival later that year, and the crowd went wild. This was the beginning of her long association with Bob Dylan.

Throughout the 1960's, Joan took a stand on many controversial issues, from war to civil rights. In 1962 Joan joined Dr. Martin Luther

King, Jr., then a thirty-three-year-old minister, in a civil rights march in Birmingham, Alabama. On November 23 of that year, *Time* magazine featured her in a cover story.

In 1963 Joan was present at the Lincoln Memorial in Washington, D.C. when Rev. King gave his historic *I Have a Dream* speech. Joan led the onlookers in her rendition of *We Shall Overcome*. Two-hundred fifty thousand people sang along with her. Joan and Bob Dylan sang duets all day long.

In 1964 Joan returned to the South to join Rev. King in another civil rights march from Selma to Montgomery, Alabama. Joan agreed with King's nonviolent approach to his plea for racial equality, and she lent her name and her voice to his cause. In the spring of 1964 and again in 1965, Joan toured with Bob Dylan to sellout crowds.

Joan continued to do as many as twenty solo concerts a year. At her shows, she would always speak out against the war in Vietnam. She had become a full-fledged antiwar activist, both onstage and offstage. In 1963 President John F. Kennedy invited Joan to sing at a White House reception. But on November 22, President Kennedy was shot and killed as his motorcade traveled through Dallas, Texas. A telegram informed Joan that the reception would still be

This was the beginning of her long association with folksinger Bob Dylan.

held, only it was to honor the new President, Lyndon B. Johnson. Joan did not like President Johnson and his policies on Vietnam. She decided to attend the reception anyway.

Dr. Martin Luther King, Jr., led a group of children to their new school in Grenada, Mississippi, in September 1966. Joan Baez joined the group.

The night was filled with fun, jokes, songs, and food. But when Joan took the floor, it was to look directly at President Johnson and tell him to listen to the youth of the nation. She said the people wanted to stay out of the war in Vietnam. Then she sang one of Bob Dylan's songs, "The Times They Are A-Changin'." Then she sang another of Dylan's songs, "Blowin' in the Wind."

JOAN BAEZ

In the fall of 1965, Joan opened a school with her longtime friend Ira Sandperl. They called the school the Institute for the Study of Nonviolence. Students were chosen on a first-come, first-served basis for a six-week term. The Institute lasted nearly a decade, later changing its name to the Resource Center for Nonviolence.

In 1966 and 1967, Joan was present on many college campuses for antiwar demonstrations and sit-ins. Hundreds upon hundreds of people showed up to protest the U.S. involvement in Vietnam and to speak out for freedom of speech. Many protesters all around the nation were jailed. Joan was sent to jail several times. During her second stay in jail, the leader of an antidraft organization called Resistance came to visit her. His name was David Harris.

David Harris had been at Stanford University in 1967 when he decided to drop out. David felt he had to leave college because college was an easy way to get out of military service. So David dropped out of school, thereby giving up his draft deferral, and then refused to be drafted. He returned his draft card and founded a draft refusal organization. He reported to his draft board to refuse induction, was put on trial, and was sentenced to jail.

After Joan got out of jail and before David went in, the two dated. David went on tour with

She said the people wanted to stay out of the war in Vietnam.

JOAN BAEZ

Joan. He was the main attraction at many of her concerts, because he was about to go to jail for his principles. Only three months after they met, they were discussing plans for marriage. On March 26, 1968, David Harris and Joan Baez were married in a church decorated with peace symbols. Joan wore a floor-length off-white dress – and no shoes.

Joan and David soon after they were married

Just a few days after they were married, a hired gunman shot and killed Martin Luther King, Jr., in Memphis, Tennessee, where King was supporting a strike by sanitation workers. Riots broke out all over the United States.

Joan and David concentrated all their efforts on Resistance. They moved to a small plot of land, which they named Struggle Mountain. They lived in a run-down house that was attached to another house. There was a large communal house nearby. The privacy that Joan had always cherished was a thing of the past.

At his trial, David was found guilty, as had been expected. In April 1969 Joan learned she was pregnant. On July 15, the sheriff showed up on Struggle Mountain, handcuffed David Harris, and took him to a federal prison in Arizona. Joan had to carry on without him.

In the summer of 1969, a music festival was held in Woodstock, New York. Woodstock had been a place for New York City artists, musicians, and writers since the early part of the century. This festival was all about peace, love, freedom, and an end to the war in Vietnam. Hundreds of thousands of people attended the music festival. Joan was six months pregnant by this time and had to take a helicopter to get there. For three days, it rained. People camped in a muddy parking lot, sharing food and blankets. Top-name performers of the day such as Crosby, Stills, Nash, and Young, Phil Ochs, and Arlo Guthrie came to sing. Joan came onstage in the middle of the night.

Joan shows off her newborn son, Gabriel, several days after he was born at Stanford Medical Center.

JOAN BAEZ

She wrote to her husband in prison every day and visited him often. But he could not be present on December 2, 1969, when their son, Gabriel, was born. David was paroled on March 15, 1971. Joan and Gabriel went to bring him home. There were photographers everywhere.

When Joan and David returned to their life together, she found it impossible to readjust. "I couldn't breathe, and I couldn't try anymore to be a wife . . . I belonged alone," Joan said. In her autobiography, she later wrote, "I am made to live alone. I cannot possibly live in the same house with anyone." In 1973 Joan and David divorced. Joan went to live in Woodside, California. David stayed in the hills, half an hour away. Gabriel traveled back and forth.

In late 1972 a Vietnamese group, the Committee for Solidarity with the American People, asked Joan Baez and three other Americans to visit North Vietnam and witness firsthand the destruction of their country in the hopes that they could revive their efforts to stop the war for good. Peace negotiations had resumed, there was a cease-fire in place for the upcoming Christmas season, and the bombing and fighting had almost stopped. So Joan agreed to tour Vietnam and deliver holiday mail to American prisoners in Hanoi.

"I am made to live alone. I cannot possibly live in the same house with anyone."

For two days, the Americans were wined and dined by their North Vietnamese hosts. They visited war memorials and schools. They were shown films about the effects of poisonous chemicals used by the U.S. in the war. It was a horrible sight. In the middle of the film, air-raid sirens wailed. The room went dark. President Richard Nixon had ordered ongoing bombing of Hanoi in a last-ditch effort to win the war.

Everyone rushed to an underground shelter. They could hear bombs exploding above them. There were ten more raids that same night. For eleven more days, the bombing continued. Joan had difficulty getting out of Vietnam. The airport had been bombed and she could not get home for Christmas. The Chinese embassy finally managed to arrange for her departure.

Joan got home to California on New Year's Day, 1973. She spent two weeks with David Harris and Gabriel, recovering and giving interviews about her visit.

In 1975 the United States, having accomplished very little, finally closed its chapter on Vietnam. By the mid-1970's folk music was no longer in style. It was considered passé. Joan was still known as a folksinger, and it took her a long time to realize that she was no longer timely. She updated her music and tried to keep her career alive. Throughout the eighties, Joan raised

By the mid-1970's folk music was no longer in style.

millions of dollars to assist people who were suffering all over the world.

In 1982 Joan performed for Peace Week, which was an appeal to put a freeze on nuclear weapons. On June 6, 1982 Joan appeared at the Rose Bowl in Pasadena, California, and urged the people to force government to change.

Joan was one of the opening acts at the Live Aid concert held in Philadelphia in July 1985.

Joan was the first performer at Live Aid held in Philadelphia in 1985 to raise money for the people of Africa. She was one of only four artists to play both Woodstock and Live Aid. "Good morning, children of the eighties!" she yelled into the microphone. "This is your Woodstock!" Then she kicked off the event with her rendition of *Amazing Grace*.

On July 11, 1988, Joan appeared at London's Wembley Stadium as part of a concert to celebrate the seventieth birthday of Nelson Mandela. Mandela, a lawyer and the political leader of South Africa's black majority, had spent most of his adult life in jail. The South African government imprisoned him for his political beliefs. Though he remained in jail for his birthday celebration, he was eventually freed in 1990.

Though she is still true to her convictions for peace, freedom of speech, and nonviolence, Joan Baez has taken a less active stand in recent years. "I'm glad I did [those things]," she told a *USA Today* reporter in April 1995, "but whatever I do from here on out will be less compulsive and more of a choice." Over the past thirty-five years, Joan has recorded more than thirty record albums, eight of which went gold. She has never stopped performing. *Diamonds and Rust,* her last big album, was released in 1975, but she has toured steadily. In 1995 she was taping four concerts for a live album due to be released in September. She now leads a quiet, single life in Woodside, California, near San Francisco, with two goats, six chickens, and a rooster. Gabriel now lives with David Harris an hour away. She says she is not through singing – yet. She acknowledges, however, what most of us already know: "I have led an extraordinary life," says Joan. It would be difficult to disagree with her.

"I'm glad I did [those things], but whatever I do from here on out will be less compulsive and more of a choice."

DISCOGRAPHY
ALBUMS BY JOAN BAEZ

Release Date	Title	Record Label
1960	*Joan Baez*	Vanguard
1960	*Folk Festival at Newport '59*	Vanguard
1961	*Joan Baez, Volume 2*	Vanguard
1962	*Joan Baez in Concert*	Vanguard
1963	*Joan Baez in Concert Part 2*	Vanguard
1964	*Joan Baez 5*	Vanguard
1965	*Farewell, Angelina*	Vanguard
1966	*Noël*	Vanguard
1967	*Joan*	Vanguard
1968	*Baptism: A Journey Through Our Time*	Vanguard
1968	*Any Day Now*	Vanguard
1969	*David's Album*	Vanguard
1969	*One Day at a Time*	Vanguard
1970	*Joan Baez – The First Ten Years*	Vanguard
1970	*Woodstock*	Cotillion
1971	*Blessed Are . . .*	Vanguard

Release Date	Title	Record Label
1972	*Big Sur Folk Festival*	Columbia
1972	*Come From the Shadows*	A & M
1973	*Hits/Greatest & Others*	Vanguard
1973	*Where Are You Now, My Son?*	A & M
1974	Gracias a la Vida	A & M
1974	*Contemporary Ballad Book*	Vanguard
1975	*Diamonds and Rust*	A & M
1976	*From Every Stage*	A & M
1976	*Gulf Winds*	A & M
1976	*Love Song Album*	Vanguard
1977	*Blowin' Away*	Portrait
1977	*Best of Joan C. Baez*	A & M
1979	*Honest Lullaby*	Portrait
1980	*Joan Baez – European Tour*	Portrait
1989	*Diamonds and Rust in the Bull Ring*	Gold Castle
1989	*Speaking of Dreams*	Gold Castle

Index

ABOUT THE AUTHOR

Barbara Marvis has been a professional writer for nearly twenty years. Motivated by her own experience with ethnic discrimination as a young Jewish girl growing up in suburban Philadelphia, Ms. Marvis developed the **Contemporary American Success Stories** series to dispel racial and ethnic prejudice, to tell culturally diverse stories that maintain ethnic and racial distinction, and to provide positive role models for young minorities. She is the author of several books for young adults, including the series **Famous People of Asian Ancestry**. She holds a B.S. degree in English and Communications from West Chester State University in West Chester, Pennsylvania, and an M.Ed. in remedial reading from the University of Delaware, in Newark, Delaware.

She and her husband, Bob, currently live with their four children in northern Maryland.